MOSQUITO

A TIN HOUSE NEW VOICE

MOSQUITO

poems

ALEX LEMON

TinHouseBooks

Published by Tin House Books, Portland, Oregon, and New York, New York
Distributed to the trade by Publishers Group West, 1700 Fourth St., Berkeley, CA 94710,
www.pgw.com

ISBN 0-9773127-4-7
First U.S. Edition 2006

Interior design by Laura Shaw Design, Inc.

www.tinhouse.com

Thanks to the editors of the following publications, where some of these poems first appeared,
sometimes in earlier versions:

AGNI: "Mosquito"; *AGNI Online 2006*: "Kinematics"; *Alaska Quarterly Review*: "Last Body";
Another Chicago Magazine: "Tumult" and "Two for My Tumor"; *Artful Dodge*: "DNA,"
"Other Good," "Preface to Augury," and "Swallowing the Scalpel"; *Black Warrior Review*:
"Love is a Very Small Tsunami"; *The Bloomsbury Review*: "The Portrait My Mother Painted
from My Mug Shot"; *Blue Collar Review*: "The Butcher Dreams"; *Butcher Shop*: "Fever"
and "Graffiti"; *Cimarron Review*: "MRI" and "The Pleasure Notebook"; *CutBank*: "The
Best Part"; *Denver Quarterly*: "Who Finds You"; *Florida Review*: "Rivets"; *Gulf Coast*:
"Scaffolding"; *Hayden's Ferry Review*: "Happy Fun Sex Movie"; *Indiana Review*: "That First
Day of Spring Kind of Feeling"; *Jabberwock Review*: "Plum"; *The Journal*: "Sophisticated";
Konundrum Engine Literary Review: "Goodbye Song"; *The Literary Review*: "Callnote";
Naranjas y Nopales: "After"; *New England Review*: "Having Been Roused . . ."; *New Orleans
Review*: "Corpus"; *Octopus*: "A Country Mile of Soft" and "The Xylophone is Blaze"; *Pleiades*:
"Cocoon," "Juke Joint," "Snow," and "Step Up"; *Post Road*: "Below the Nearer Sky" and "Silt";
Salt Hill: "Fantastic Goes the Lost Cause"; *Sonora Review*: "Happiness"; *Swink*: "Ashtray";
Tin House: "Look Close"; *Typo*: "Mugging"; *Washington Square*: "Trembling"

— For Ma —

CONTENTS

3.

4.

INTRODUCTION

"Physical pain," Elaine Scarry writes in *The Body in Pain*, her brilliant examination of the intersection of suffering, language, and power, "does not simply resist language but actively destroys it, bringing about an immediate reversion to a state anterior to language, to the sounds and cries a human being makes before language is learned."

How does pain erase speech? First, of course, because the one doing the hurting is too englobed in the experience of hurt to make any words: hit your thumb with a hammer and it's as if the bone-deep intensity of that experience hijacks all energy from the mind; nothing can be seen or felt but the throbbing, blinding "this-ness" of that experience. As if there were nothing in the world but ache.

Throbbing, blinding, ache: the relative paucity of the words themselves point to the second reason why pain eludes the saying. We don't have the vocabulary for it. English, which has an endless supply of terms for, say, getting drunk, offers the barest scraps to help us name the way we're ailing. Pain can be throbbing, stabbing, shooting, piercing, or burning, and that's about it. Is this because intoxication is primarily a social experience, whereas pain is the opposite, always experienced alone? Words exist for the realm of the shared. Our poverty of terms for pain may indicate that we've given up on creating a lexicon, understanding that the solitary, suffering subject remains a solitary. When we are wordless, we tend to be world-less as well. What cannot be conveyed about the self and the body lodges stubbornly in either silence or "sounds and cries."

But poetry is unlike other language, and its difference from daily speech lies in part in its relationship to those wordless utterances. Poetry bases itself in the sheer expressive power of vowel and consonant; rhythmic, bodily sound-making; moan and exhalation; the outcry that shades into song. Stanley Kunitz says that his poems begin in sound, and "sense has to fight its way in." The music that lies beneath speech is a vehicle of feeling.

Perhaps it's this grounding in the physicality of language that gives poetry its courage to wrestle with the difficult, if not downright impossible, work of getting the barely sayable onto the page. Poetry's power exists in exact proportion to this attempt; the harder it tries to do what can't be done, the more beautiful and engaging its failure. Or perhaps better to say that its failure—the inability of words to be commensurate with the power of experience—begins to come out the other side, and somehow or other, through some feat of linguistic legerdemain, a poem is made that does what speech shouldn't be able to do. A miraculous poem approximates the character of subjectivity, how it is to be in the world.

Alex Lemon's "Other Good" seems to me a miraculous poem, one that locates a vocabulary for a near-unspeakable realm of experience. Here is its opening passage:

> Anesthesia dumb, scalpel-paste
> Rawing my tongue, I found
> Myself star-fished in sky
> Spinning days. I stared into my eyelids'
>
> Bustling magic, the black
> Of my hands. Oh, how darkness
> Swaggered, dealt fluorescent-blurs
> & the choke of the sea. *This is my everything—*
>
> Bright shuddered my cheeks,
> Shadows whistled through their teeth,
> Hallways thrummed & snorted,
> The surgeons in my brain
>
> Pissed with no hands.

The poem's first and considerable accomplishment is to de-familiarize the hospital world: no familiar furniture here, no IV bottles and cranked-up beds with white-white sheets. Lemon's unexpected image-world immediately evokes the speaker's disorientation and ravishment, and the reader is swiftly desta-bilized and placed into a linguistic territory that is the result, at least metaphorically, of that "rawing" of the tongue; it isn't possible to speak in "cooked," orderly terms here, not when

you're "starfished in sky / Spinning days."
    The poem continues:

Each day nurses wore their best
Tinfoil skirts, buried
Their caresses in my side

While pillows whispered
In spite of your scars you are tickled
To death   of life.
I couldn't understand this

Always being held. Lung-machines
Sang louder. Wave song & useless.
Midnights & swearing. Blue.

It's a wonderful, unexpected turn, what those pillows have to
say; this is no moment when we'd expect to meet an affirma-
tion. But thc flesh wants to live: the body's greatest impera-
tive is to continue. That line and stanza break after "I couldn't
understand this" is cunningly placed; it makes us read the line
as a part of the sentence before and of the sentence below.
In other words, I couldn't understand why I'd be happy to
live, and I couldn't understand this "always being held," the
caresses, the engines and practices of care bearing the speaker
through difficulty.
    It's telling, too, how syntax breaks apart here, sentences
growing shorter and shorter as the forceful verbs that are part
of this poet's signature fall away. Now we're floating in a state

where time (and its vehicle, the sentence) has been atomized. "Wave song & useless. / Midnights & swearing. Blue." In the depth of the body's night, we're suspended in mere fragments of speech, all that can be voiced here.

And now the poem enters its final moments:

Who prayed for me—my thanks

But I can't keep anything down.
Who knew it had nothing to do
With the wind by how light
Flickered with falling knives?

No easy affirmation there; the speaker can't keep down, presumably, food *or* prayers. The light outside the window is itself dangerous; the world's a treacherous place, and yet the creaturely self relishes being alive in it. We're taken right back to the italicized passage, midpoem, with its key line: *"To death of life."* Here the poem's central terms are placed in bald opposition, both linked and separated by the space/silence/caesura between them; they're the two poles of the world, the inseparable north and south of things, yes and no, one and zero.

What keeps this affirmation believable and vital is, of course, how realistically guarded it is; the speaker may be *"tickled / To death"* to be alive, but it's the knives that have the last word. Though here knives might be said to be good things; aren't they the instruments of the speaker's delivery? He tells us, after all, in "The Best Part," that the "sweetest ingredient" of brain surgery "is the cutting. Hollow space / that longs to be filled with what little I have." Even that violation of the creaturely self has a beauty to it; the opening of the self points to the possibility that it might be filled with something else.

But it's not simply polarity that makes Lemon's poem an amulet and charm against the speechlessness of suffering. The harnessing of opposites is, instead, a characteristic of his style, which is the agency of his magic.

Style, that amalgam of the found and the made, the improvised and the adapted, can be the meeting ground between self and world. A means of self-presentation is forged, and in doing so the contents of individual experience can be signaled, given shape. The pain of others—just like their joy or pleasure or wit or desire—can remain entirely invisible to us unless it is given utterance, but plainspoken language generally fails to carry much of a depth charge. Not long ago, at a university in the north of England, a reader asked me if I couldn't just come out and *say* things; did I need the appurtenances of metaphor, the fancy dress of linguistic performance? No matter that to state how I'm feeling or thinking might take me a sentence or three, and not necessitate the several books of poetry and prose that she had neatly stacked on the desk in front of her, their pages marked with colored Post-it notes.

No, the crucial thing was that I couldn't say "it," because when named directly, abstractly, "it" vanishes. The subjective world can't be rendered in a summation: "I nearly lost my life but now I am better," Alex Lemon might say, but so what? That statement might move us in conversation, but on the page it's empty. It is the made machinery of style that manages to replicate how it feels to be alive, and that's why we require it. "I stared into my eyelids' / Bustling magic," Lemon writes instead, "the black / Of my hands. Oh, how darkness / Swaggered, dealt fluorescent-blurs / & the choke of the sea." That is direct, in its way, but it's also thoroughly couched in style, a mode of speaking.

"This is how it must be to make a language," Sandra McPherson writes in "Suspension: Junior Wells on a Small Stage in a Converted Barn," a beautiful poem occasioned by listening to the blues musician Junior Wells. She should know. Like Wells, she makes her signature sound out of the found and the improvised, cobbling together variation and synthesis, working out an idiom that will stand in for the texture of subjectivity, a model of the perceiving and speaking self. Like the blues, the making of a poetic style is a triumph over speechlessness, a refiguring of the dynamics of power, a song—however flinty and peculiar—where none had seemed possible.

Style, unlike the defenseless body it is meant to clothe and to present, has a sort of permanence. John Berryman's poems, for instance, which must be one of the ingredients of Lemon's own wrought aesthetic, feel imbued with a sense of personality, the particular quirks of wit and bitterness. The regret and longing that fuel them are just as palpable now as they were the day the poems were written. Selfhood vanishes; style persists. As Berryman did, Lemon likes heated verbs, diction shifts ("thrummed" and "pissed"), tonal variations, a quick joke, outbursts of lyricism; he likes a poem to speed down the page. His artfully deployed stanzaic forms orchestrate our movement through his poems, arranging silences into patterns, making a music for ear and eye. He weaves a quick-shifting fabric of figurative speech that seems to keep the poem fluid, unstable. Alex Lemon makes something larger than any narration of personal experience: a container for struggle, love, and delight—even, for the wounded and dumb body ("anonymous as graffiti"), an undeceived, adult form of hope.

—*Mark Doty*

Trembling

Hello friend, beautiful face
in car fire. I, the flesh wish,
am sickly wrapped in light.

I promise to wink the voyeur,
spike the drinks to a fine glow
& swallow. What happened
to your arms? Raw concrete,

bad paint? Uncapped, the bottle
can't be broken. Voice, be amazing
circling the river bottom.

Remember fingers rattling locks,
fingers jump-starting the zipper
spine. Filleted boy. Anesthesia
is the bottle rocket. The belly.

Did you hear the rain last night,
thunder? Tomorrow, I will be
afraid. I might never wake up.

I

MRI

An old man is playing fiddle in my head.
At least that's what the doctor says,
pointing, as he holds my MRI to the light.

He must be eating the same hot dogs
my nephew microwaves. My nephew sees
Bob the Builder everywhere—smiling

in sauerkraut, sawing in the drifting sky.
Afternoons he names me Bob, knocks
my knee with a plastic hammer. I'm half-

naked, shivery with chicken skin,
napkin-gowned. But I don't laugh
because I think the veined cobweb

looks like Abe Lincoln's profile on the penny.
So let's pretend I'm not sick at all.
I'm filled with golden tumors—

love for the nurse who feeds me
to the machine. The machine worse
than any death—the powerlessness

of a shaved & strapped-down body.
Even in purgatory you can wear earrings
& though the music might crack a spine,

at least in that torture, the tears from your arm's
needle marks are mouth-wateringly sweet.

The Best Part

The best part of brain surgery isn't the shining
staples that keep it all in, the ways

fingers and tongues will find the scar.
It's not wheelchair rides through maple leaves,

sunlight warming a bruise as I fumble
peeling an orange. Nor is it the gentle tug

of a nurse reminding muscles—bend, stretch
and flex. The sweetest ingredient—

the best part is the cutting. Hollow space
that longs to be filled with what little I have.

The first bite, cold fruit. Bedridden, I weigh
my glass eye in a wrinkle-mapped hand.

After

i.

Open my mouth & watch the mouse-trapped shake,
　　the maggot-house-meat

　　　　　　　　　splayed before dogs—I am
　　that scab

peeled from the butcher's midnight eyes.

　　　　　　　　　Persistent scalpel—I will thorn soft

these ill-illuminated pleasures.

　　　　　　　　　The mouth whips. The mouth
　　　　　　　　　whips itself clean with wind.

ii.

I knife your words into trees & repeat them backwards

　　　　　　　　　to feel, thieve ear to breast
　　　　　　　　　like a cheat. Today I hunger

for the smallest sheen, hunger for leaves backboning
    a chain-link fence.

                      A shattered-foot ballerina, I cross
                      pavement split-

lipped, slopping my ruby hooves. Birthing children

                      piece by piece, I live by fortune
                      cookies, blizzards & scars.

Two for My Tumor

Incantation mumbling in the cutting
room, I watch hooks blossom

with corrugated beef—imagine the chunk
they towed from the sawed-bone bowl

of my skull. At night, I swallow
thousands of fists—gasp when lightning

splinters winter sky. Every splitting
rib cage whispers—*Now, goddamn it.*

Right fucking now. It's time to pay for stealing
only a scar from the larder's shearing light.

———

The morning saw squeals
through rock-hard chickens

as I scribble with the tip
of a blade. What is left—

savor child dog marrow—
The body's secrets should be

anonymous as graffiti
in bathroom stalls, brilliant

as sun-chromed snow. Today,
I see like a drowned man, bait whirling

radiant as stars in a pierced sky,
sea-grass bowing to greet.

Scaffolding

It would take jackhammers
to find that other-self. Saw-shrieks,

elegies for taste—whiplash,
moan & scald. This body

is something Giacometti
sculpted: wax & molten steel,

the die-cast of night's necessities.
Smaller, I beg you, smaller.

For fear my outline is neither
live nor dead, air dances electric

with broken ghosts. Cheeks
absent of color: lip after the bite.

⁓

Sticky in autumn's poplar, the voyeur,
who may or may not be me, sketches
the leaf's cursive fall. Grasshoppers sleep

in amber. This could be feeling: not good,
but at least not hurt. I need spells & voodoo

to stop time. Close my eyes—bring me
willing things, orphans waiting open-armed
for needles, gravel-floored cellars & spiders
the size of fists. Underwater, you cannot hear

my favorite song: a mouth whispering
half my name, all the sheets turned down.

Last Body

—after Mark Conway

Please me when I say take it
For a ride—make it a place others
Might understand. Let me explain—

A prairie puzzled apart by lightning
For example, the oak vamping de-limbed
In winter, or how each pair of tennis shoes is

Unwound from the power line. But none of this
Shines like a rain of thumbtacks. For a mouth
Open is no different than frostbite or a bucket of bolts

Slopping into the sun's bath. It is a barking animal
But do not say dog. I will check for the baby
Beneath my dress. Now, we have highways

& nothing seems far enough away. The way
Of holy eyes—morning & knife-in-the-box
That act of misunderstanding, which is

Much more casual than a glass dusted in sunlight
& because we call it casual, or a glass in sunlight
It will not break or bleed. This is fundamental

& nothing came before. I adore you the blizzard
That going blank, that's fine. A raccoon
Awake & thief-mouthed in the dumpster

The half-chewed chicken bone is a truth
That little victim is suffer everything & joy

DNA

You have to admit, pushing my wheelchair
was better than painting my dead lips.

Maybe, the surgeon said, caressing my head
like a hurricane. I wished I was a tan girl, hands

overflowing with perfect shells. You needn't
ask, Mother, I forgive you. Stop nailing yourself to trees.

Pray my child never has to fall asleep cold,
waiting to be cut by strangers. Give them nothing

of mine, I'll tell them before they shake
a heart to life in a test tube. Science:

make it red hair, brown eyes,
& by the way, Mother, the market

where we cried biting apples, *Whole
Foods*—they don't let me in there anymore.

Goodbye Song

I've hummed it so many times I can't feel
the right side of my face & now

I'd rather be gagged with guitar strings
& dragged behind a hot rod than sit

deadlog in a wheelchair. How many times
will you push a needle into my thigh

before something more brilliant
wakes? O, whistling skin of a pierced

& patched body. I stumble through life
like a kicked dog. How many have dropped

wishes in my skull? Dipped,
then pressed wet-tipped fingers

to their lips? When the body quakes
& pink bubbles crawl lips, push

the chest down—squeeze & plunge the knife
so the tongue is frozen & bit.

Swallowing the Scalpel

The hospital's bell-throat moans
as my roommate dies. Remembering

where the goodbye letters were hidden,
the scarred clatter spoons in the hall.

Doctors gulp, click their teeth—
hum when skin accepts the cutting.

Tomorrow my head opens. If I am still
here, someone let me know what I am.

⌒

Paint a still life of my pillow. Use red. Be messy.
Remember the time you rode to the fields,

watched the calf work itself frothy in barbed wire.
Scribble that churning, the emptying of wails.

Remember how the dissected cat leaked
its chorus of sweet end? Shade in the hunger—

the not keeping anything down. Remember sheets
scabbed with stains. Pull out your hair, rub the fibers in.

Dip your fingers in the toilet and flick. Remember to scrape
a blade to best show what stuck during the night.

———

These pills are a lover sneering *motherfucker*.

Melted lungs, oil smoking from a lathe. Too many,
and moths waterfall from nostrils, nuzzle the body's graffiti.
They are the last gasps of a premature baby.

Rattle them off my teeth, let's pass them with our tongues.

———

I would have handcuffed myself to a bumper, jumped
from a bridge to feel my lungs. But I watched the seasons

from a wheelchair. Doctors fed me steroids, stretched
my legs. A nurse scrubbed me clean. Months passed

before they wrapped my fingers around a cane.
During winter's first flurry I dropped everything—

spun half-drunk away from my mother, cane standing
as if held by the dark sky—and ran like a storm cloud

before falling into the slush. Overturned, my eye patch filled
with snow, lay like a mirror that would never show my face.

I shave my head because my eyes are monks swallowing
their tongues, and only hunching at a table

in a bookstore can make me whole. *The Lorax*,
Where the Wild Things Are, children point openmouthed

at scars. They buy with jars of dimes.
Read books where fat words lumber the page

like headlights illuminating a pharmaceutical fog.
I hum in my corner, hoping for more time—

for them to choke on the gasp of a body kicking
back to life—for a nurse to wicked their tiny muscles

raw. Smiles anesthesia-dark, their eyes flash like razors
that let snowflakes slice, cold as surgical steel.

2

God, whom I've so often offended, has spared me this time;
at the moment when I am writing these lines a quite exceptional
storm has just been making the most terrible ravages.

—PAUL GAUGUIN

Love Is a Very Small Tsunami

When I spin fast enough, my socks
fling into the rough and burning world
like gasoline-dipped bees or the dirty tube
socks they are. Which really means I'm lonely
and have a garden of meticulous succulents.
My cactus lips slap fables of sleep
on trees. Pigeons play in my mouth.
The day is all sky and it's not even
January or midnight. Little mouse,
come out come out. If you drink
from my hand the Lord will not lend
me a shovel. Oh furry gray sun,
life is all bloody sheets. Leaf-hearted,
I won't eat eggs or peas, but slam tequila
shots until my eyes are cheeks and wet
as piss buckets. I eat with my hands.
No forks. No spoons. Knives only
for afternoons at the ballet where I stab
myself so I can streak, howl into the apple-
rotting sunlight. Sunlight where the gumball
is the only prayer I need. I race to the lake
where bodies drown in algae and the mind
flexes everything naked. Without coming up,
I swim to the lilacs where homeless snarl
orchestras from garbage cans and weep
grease-eyed when brushed by tan skin.

I use torque like a jellyfish.
I think shark fin and ladle.
When my toes kiss the shore,
it's usually raining. I'm hungry and exhausted.
I crave bacon on my bagel and you
are always smiling when I wet-dog it
to the counter. On that day you watch me
chew, you'll realize I've always lived upstairs,
apartment thumpy with music and flushing toilets.
Shuddering, you'll swoon with the thought
of bacon and when the heart begins to sweat,
thread will pull from your jeans, drawn to my face
passing in the window, where sweetly,
it will rumble into the ideogram for disaster.

Plum

You shook, rolled clothes from hips like the sea,
circling arms in a friction I thought would burn
our home and before I could say a little bit of hail,
you were sitting buckass naked on the couch,
where your wetness stuck, cried, like a mouse
in a glue trap and you didn't begin. Not yet.
Instead, beads of sweat ran your body
and we stared in complete silence at the fruit dish:
oranges, apples and plums like the google-eyed audience
of a solar eclipse removing welding glasses,
and even the baby's wails could not pull us
from our meditation and then I saw your birthmark
sitting between your breasts and it is, in fact,
the seventh president. An earring had fallen
and you'd picked it up with your toes where it hung
from that delicate wing of flesh like it had pierced
and I could see the patch of hair you'd missed shaving
glow on your calf like a gold brick in an Iowa cornfield
and drowning in this ecstasy I remembered waking
to song, you sloshing in the tub, water flooding
the tile as you flailed against morning, groaning
lyrics I would swear were Dylan's but just
as your keys caressed the door that afternoon, I heard
that song, and it turns out it is just some guy trying
to sound like Dylan and by the time the fake had finished,
you were half-undressed, trembling, hypnotizing me

with your bones, the sound of rain on the sofa.
Your lips moved, and I stopped you, put a finger
in the air like I had an idea that could save the world
or a secret I swore to tell but instead, unmoving, I sat
like a jackass, finger in the air, and you,
beautifully naked and absolute, smiling
away my incompetence, shaking your head
and biting a plum, juice streaking to your chin,
dripping like steam condensing on the shower mirror.

Fantastic Goes the Lost Cause

—for SY

A week & we crawl. We lisp.
Soaked in shine, the crooked
I am fine. *In my head*
turns progressions idle.
Steady wick the livid clouds.

We print names in blood
on white T-shirts. Scratch
steady to shine. Moonlight
confounds us nasty & the heart
murmurs. Baggies of ash, mothball

white. It used to be & it is. Steady
arm, go steady. The beginning begins
& someone cries—you shouldn't know
how. Infinite desolation & shine.
Come steady, let's drive all night.

We'll sing the get by & broken
will press from our lips. Dawn
is always a fistfight, don't be afraid.
Purity is butterfly-stomached & pallid.
Purity will never find a place so divine.

The Pleasure Notebook

I

Bend closer—taste the thumbprint mirror, lick a bit
    of struck-match mercy

Shadow-laced & red, light helps splinter the cruelty met with
    a flayed body

—

What named me, the moth pleads, banging jazz
    from lightbulbs

        Whose flash can raw a perfect face?
        Meaning is the glistening cobweb
        Smooth, a spider's deceptive legs

—

I need breath thick with fire, syrup spilled from a swollen
    heart

I need bites promising grace. Luminous, a tongue that prays
    for wounds

2

　　　　　　Naked shapes devour winter light
They sizzle, salt the topography of despair

Stare & the body's brittle math twists into uncertainty
　　　　　　　Mime-lips mashing sleet-swept cheeks

⌒

I say nothing in defense of the hand

But praise drool's fine silk stringing from a thigh

The furred wing wrenched off in honey

⌒

A static-voice hammers thick over the leafless tree's growling

Sheets are sap-streaked like bark

Tonight—brass-knuckled love, weep & birthmarks break
　　from the self

3

I don't care that you sleep on your stomach, groaning
　　fortune-cookie koans all night

The limb's edged knots & I come just thinking of you

Emperor of gasps, paradise of sweaty face

—

Feed me the slow lesson of flowers, plum pits knocking
    teeth & dark

My skin is everyone's magic trick. How couldn't it be?

What sad-luck damage would you trade for taste?

—

Melodies drill deep wells in the chest

4

As a child I worshipped chains worming through gravel. But
    now

Is sugar from a heartwormed pit bull, benediction slaps
    from tattooed gods

—

Kiss my reflection into brick walls, carve me golden & throaty

5

Streets are gorgeous with pissing dogs, red-petal tongues
& grandfather cartwheeling with muscled legs

He didn't feel the heart's disintegration
on the slick tile floor. A percussive

axe cracking the bathroom door. Bleached radio
piercing the sun with a tune I'll never remember

6

Touch the photo that peels clothes. Hunger for it like bare
    feet

On sun-slivered pavement, cricket legs longing for rubs

Slip me into that train-track bed, torsos weaving

Wicked & blue. City of fence-rust, streetlights bulling for life

Lopsided with fog, what must passengers think staring
    down dawn?

Bodies arched into something only sewers can name

            Orchard of polished ghosts, flesh pimpled
            with rain

Teeming wordless & terrible, grief dangles
from concrete fruit

7

My yard is frail with crushed cans, flat-sailed rubbers

It is the felled redbreast's grass-jawed grave

Bottle caps like diamonds buried in a finger-box of ribs

⁓

Jigsaw morning, the branch hisses mud

⁓

Trodden & cubist. Too much gesso & not enough light

Paint my nothing portrait, use amphetamines

Paint the gift of the neon wasp

⁓

It is the year of the dismembered horse
Bury me with bone-dice instead of eyes

Juke Joint

I'd strip, peel myself to show you
the jukebox of hearts. Still,
you'd frown, say that's nothing—
a foot pressed into river mud,
movie dialogue edited for TV
where the bad guy turns cotton
candy. Boxer-veins streaking
his forehead, he aims the pistol,
shucks, he says, mouth twisted
into fuck. Don't stop listening,
it's a train chugging runaway
on ecstasy. Overflowing fishbowl
or uncovered cage, you'd ask,
ear to my ribs like a doctor.
You'd point everywhere,
confused until I tell you,
I am hi-fi, all of me is surround
sound. I snap fingers & the world
is xylophones. Feel my wrist,
it is a coda dragging its feet. I click
my teeth like cymbals. Hold
your hand to my chest, I'll baptize you
in the river. But we have to start
now. Here—take off my belt.

A Country Mile of Soft

Do it, the river wept
this morning. *No one will*

know. I burned
the autographs.

Licked crayon-wax
from my fingers

to celebrate waking.
I wallpapered nude

so when I flipped
into the down-dog,

I became the jumping
bean's slow cousin.

This is the New West.
The la-la in sagebrush,

a magic-strummed scenery.
Last night was guns & confetti,

an elephant-sized centrifuge & we
were spic & span, tongued safe & clean.

Happiness

does not keep him from feeling
the woman within kick and claw.
His habits are not his alone.
Behind the sunglasses' missing lens,
an eye blinks sunburnt. He reaches
with perfect manners, right arm
stealing tomatoes from the salad.
Left sleeve sewn to his side, he is spill-proof,
enjoys tart wine in chiming glass.
Locked away, a shoe befriends half a scissor,
collects pecks from a lonesome lovebird.
A pant sleeve pinned above the knee,
he looks as if he's been jumping
one-legged in floodwater, saving
only one of the twins. He wears
the up-all-night face of singles tennis,
orders individual knives from infomercials.
One sock. One nostril. One glove. One arm.
Wave to him when he holds nothing.
At happy hour watch him handle the two for one.

Step Up

Welcome to the carnival
of misfortune, drunks singing

in sweat-thick air. Howling
like locusts, they point at stars,

map the never coming home.
Believe me when I tell you

I've stolen everything.
Have a goldfish, I am yearning

to share the moon. Billiard balls clack
& cars groan away. Eight-ball,

side pocket & the ghost-ring
doorbell. Under streetlights,

touch is pyrotechnic Braille.
The blues are crumbling—fiddle,

hawkweed & horn. Blow that
trumpet, baby, use my spit.

Graffiti

i.

We litany the air with bottle caps, swallow
slivers of glass & rend our names. Husked-cathedrals

of horseflies purple & flash, rattle the headlights'
dusk. Skinnings from their bites piled high.

ii.

The choke-collared dog pants its music.
Coke machine, concrete, a freckled boy
shoots gumballs into the shadows.

Hold your breath & it isn't impossible
to hear the bent-back fingers. Coat hanger—
blade-song fashioning bone.

iii.

Nostrils ringed golden, a girl snorts baggies of spray paint
& her heart freezes—confused & thick with pleasure. Pallets

for sleep, box cutters for midnight. Her lovers spit
by the dumpsters—blame luck & stroll, all switchblade lips.

iv.

The radiators burst irresistibly. Press for me packs
        of ice—I will never feel. Go deeper,
the sky booms when I tear open—

the man across the way whipping dishes
        from his third-story window. Bawls & begging
for more rising from the stagger-throated street.

Desideratum

—*after Michael Burkard*

One potato, two potato, me potato whore—
And then we bang, and I realize
This whole time, we've had the entire dilemma
Upside down and we must unknot
Our bodies. Already, I feel our bowel-
Heavy needs calcifying into gallstones
For it is the same failure of light
Each noon. The same squirrel, red lighting
At the window. Of course we'll continue
To brand each other with hope
That someone might deliver us a murder
Of stone-stunned crows. That we might hold them
To our ears and hum along with the muted conversation
That is not the sea but the pitchfork
Of our happiness pushing in and out
Of oil-sopped hay. The fire alarm will still sing
And my pacemaker will still shrug—
And like good little kiddies we'll crouch
Below our desks and cover
Each other's groins, confident
That our heartbeats' zings
Are just giggles in the bestiary of our desires.
We'll pinch and grimace our flesh-
Eating pleasures, not wavering
In our mumbled odes to catastrophe
Only a teensy bit afraid to go on

The Portrait My Mother Painted from My Mug Shot

It's old canvas—rotted wood & splinter,
paint shattered like ice. My face is a riot

of flake & line. After the accident, the cops
pistol-whipped me empty—I was chipped-

teeth, eyes like megaphones. Over me lay
a darker stillness, a sheet of red silk. She took

that blood. You can't smell the singed hair.
She made pitch & range with pigment

& brushstroke. Face without swelling, eyes
nothing but blue. She squeezed melody

from my bruises. Hold the mug shot next
to the frame & I look like I fathered myself.

Mosquito

You want evidence of the street
fight? A gutter-grate bruise & concrete scabs—
here are nails on the tongue,
a mosaic of glass shards on my lips.

I am midnight banging against house
fire. A naked woman shaking
with the sweat of need.

An ocean of burning diamonds
beneath my roadkill, my hitchhiker
belly fills sweet. I am neon blind & kiss
too black. Dangle stars—

let me sleep hoarse-throated in the desert
under a blanket sewn from spiders.
Let me be delicate & invisible.

Kick my ribs, tug my hair.
Scream *you're gonna miss me*
when I'm gone. Sing implosion
to this world where nothing is healed.

Slap me, I'll be any kind of sinner.

3

Other Good

Anesthesia dumb, scalpel-paste
Rawing my tongue, I found
Myself starfished in sky
Spinning days. I stared into my eyelids'

Bustling magic, the black
Of my hands. Oh, how darkness
Swaggered, dealt fluorescent-blurs
& the choke of the sea. *This is my everything—*

Bright shuddered my cheeks,
Shadows whistled through their teeth.
Hallways thrummed & snorted,
The surgeons in my brain

Pissed with no hands.
Each day nurses wore their best
Tinfoil skirts, buried
Their caresses in my side

While pillows whispered
In spite of your scars you are tickled
To death   of life.
I couldn't understand this

Always being held. Lung-machines
Sang louder. Wave song & useless.
Midnights & swearing. Blue.
Who prayed for me—my thanks

But I can't keep anything down.
Who knew it had nothing to do
With the wind by how light
Flickered with falling knives?

Slake

All morning I've watched puddles
Strain. Down the street, a hammer's tremolo

On steel—the many ways we've failed.
Each time a door opens I hear a child

Choking. I wave into mirrors
And there he is—swallowing fistfuls

Of pills. In tonight's brambled-dark,
He will kiss the first stranger he sees

With an open mouth. Shirt torn,
Desire calligraphied from lips—

No matter what we wish, he'll shiver,
It will all jackhammer on—

Rivers yearning for the eye-blank sky as it whispers
Its tender needles, its gluttony of clouds.

Fuck You Lazy God

—for Nick Flynn

Be afraid my blissful numbskulls
    You are mine   Plead

Your *asshole* & *amen* but
    Like blackouts I have perfect

Timing   I cannot suffer for you
    Lips glistening with honey

Because there is a man
    Behind my ribs break dancing

His spin—glide—split
    A choir of meat hooks humming

Their hi-fi heaven   Now can you see
    How it will end   All of it slick

With the breath I lose each night
    When they scalpel me open

& from the mirrored hive of my throat—
    My arrows my Eros my errors

Tongue swarming bone-black—
  Red-glisten-red—head

Blossoming with bruise

Mugging

I.

This is chipped-teeth, the kicked-heart,
dried blood on grandfather's blanket.

> I stretch to not be strangled
> by the eleventh breath.

The body is a rotting orchard, eyes of cracked wings.

In the yard, the neighbor's dog, all red sores
> & ribs, face an instrument
> of torture, looks to my window,
> hollow mouth broken by light.

> Nothing is permanent.
> Nothing lives in this bed.

Steam floats from my shoulders like breath.

Naked, I wait to be tuned like a fallen god's
flute. Cadence of a rattling shower
> thumping my bruise. The music
> of not knowing fills me, the too sweet
> meat of an animal not yet dead.

II.

Is there still time for me to stop
shivering under the purple weight
of a plum, palm trembling
beneath the supermarket's brilliance?

I wanted to pull it cleanly away,
peel flesh until I found a layer sweet
in pain. My tongue flicked tender corners,
caught rivers of blood in a pool
so deep it could fill lungs.

I still walk this poorly lit block
past midnight, vision filled
with bodies split into floods.
On these streets where black eyes expand
like nebulae, I refuse to understand
exploding shadows, how physics
carves gentle lines, a mural's scar.
But somewhere in this gesture
I have come to realize the stupidity
of most of this world's wants.
Recesses of the body caked
with blood, the fine art of stains.

Little Handcuffs of Air

The streetlights will blush when I sing

I felt a funeral in my brain, dragging

My car-struck dog until worms spill

From his asphalt-shorn heart

And I weep—my voice emptying

Into the twirling dark like a house fire

For I am busted-lipped and scurvy

Thorned skin glowing   *Kiss my spokes*

But always it will be never   It will be too late and lustrous

Into me lightning everywhere and you lovely

And leaching out of our chests   All of us

Coming   Anvil-tongued   We will be

Sundered with light

Kinematics

Someone is hanging from an ice pick
Wrestled into my lung
But I haven't had Blue Cross
In so long it might only be my memory
Of a blue jay chasing the others away—
House finch, sparrow and pigeon—
How it sat at the feeder,
Beak-high, without eating for hours.
The entire afternoon I watched, reliving
The smoke-dark morning I shot my best friend,
And how four years later, seniors
In high school, we sat drunk on Pabst,
Squeezing the remaining buckshot from his calf
As a girl we both thought was ours
Watched, a cigarette burning a knuckle
On her hand. The moon was something
I will never remember and plutonium
Was what I thought of the fireflies.
And now, when I leave my porch
The ground will give beneath my feet
On this day wet and comfortable
With warm rain. Most of the apples are mealy
With bruises, but I will sliver them
With my grandfather's pocketknife, eat
Them with peanut butter while sipping green tea.

It would be much easier if I could
Say I have so much of everything I don't
Remember loving anything at all, but really,
What wouldn't I do for twenty bucks?

Rivets

I cannot help but sing survival by stumbling
Slick-chested along the river, each floating can
Promising an avenue of catfish. Dark

Wheat of gilded water—the cure of a mouth
Gasping. & above, the street bridge fills with voice
& the smack of doors slamming. Again & another & so on

To infinity. So the tanager on the park bench. So the stoplight
Dizzying red. Cars like old bulls limp around icy corners
& I am simple, knitting myself from this barbed-wire wind

It cannot be called "after" because there is still snow
& our eyes are hard & unblinking. I confess this system
Of hazy skylines—fast-moving constellations of shouts

Plastic bags are like clouds & you are a necessary-mouthed
Dumpster. The barges clang or an explosion in the sky
It has been a kung-fu winter, months of rat-thick pillows

But this midnight the deal is different, huzzah, huzzah—
Your grace is half plague, your hands are full of shaking

Ashtray

When the paramedics kicked his heart
back to life—the blooming light, doctors
cutting away his vocal cords, a lung—
Grandpa heard children tearing
through leaves. I promised not to tell anyone
about the flowerpot filled with ash,
the yellow-walled smell. I caressed his back
with a warm washcloth. Vibrator at his throat,
he buzzed his pleasure. Kneading skin
in silence, I traveled the universe
on his tattoos. Mountains and ships—acres
of faded ink. I rubbed circles, pushed
until his back roared, the ocean of his gravel-
skinned shoulder blade where a woman,
naked and fierce, dangled from an anchor,
winking her secrets: there is never a reason for fear,
simple as the crashing wave—Grandpa's smile
as tumors turned him slowly into night.
How he held the X-ray to the window,
inhaling a cigarette through the hole in his throat
until it blazed, bright as an eye.

Silt

—after Charles Baxter

In the dark, I count fingers,
Watch lightning spider
Over the mountain's toothy peaks.

All the while, the cupola grows
Cloudy with accidents—
Dark blossoms sticky and wet,

Clinging shadowy with reincarnation.
Yesterday eight and, now, eleven
Memories distilled, frayed.

The neck-breaking spiral
Of this morning's junco
Landing on a gnarled fence,

A surgeon's fingers tapping
His way through afternoon sleep,
Breaking a heart into ballet

Or the several postures of pain
A body makes falling unconscious
In the bathroom while violins roar

On a television straining with blue
Light. The fatigue of healing
Interrupted by the susurrus

Of an empty shower. An ear, blood-
Smeared cheek and bit lip—
A sterile, sweating tiled floor.

Having Been Roused by the Sound of a Garbage Truck from a Moment of Unwaking in Which a Fishing Hook Is Pulled from My Hand by the Mouth of My Grandfather

On the boulevard, morning's cottonous haze hunches—
Already hot breath & car exhaust among the dahlias.
Stumbling to the trash can, the neighbor's wave unbuckles
The sky. These are the beautiful ways we exist—rain needling
His sweatshirt, light orange-stripping from above. & blocks
Away, to the beer-bottled river where a wading man shouts
To a stray dog. His hands, bleeding & pruned, sweep suck-
Holes for cans—the same man having followed someone
He loves home last night. The same man who stared into a
Half-lit window, drenched in a midnight heat. This insomnia
Is more deafening than the buzz. Cracks moaning when
You walk that same water during winter's deep freeze. More
Important than the head-tilt when watching your pickup
Wrap around a phone pole. Headlights are always
Swerving now. Not yet, they flash, not just yet. Soon there
Will be digging in the lilacs. Boots will pit the thicket. Soon
Will be the simmer, the hollow of failing fruit.

The Butcher Dreams

Butcher paper, breasts, fresh snow.
I hacked whole flocks of chicken,
blade orange with rust.

We swung slabs of beef
from hooks. Heavy shadows
dripping through freezers, steam.

White aprons hungry for blood,
we used our weight to split
ribs, break bones.

Moans, the ripping of our saws.
We struggled, pink fingers,
pork against glass.

Late into night, I'd lie exhausted.
Weary brain unfolding
like a lotus, intricate map of the heart.

Arpeggio

Outside the smoking & beard-burdened trees—
    & always again, it is winter

Always again children streak into traffic, & again, & always,
    I'm decapitated

& feel   as though   someone is lip-tracing

The zippers of my self-inflicted bites   & it is true—
    the only thing I can

Fully understand about sickness is a tractor dragging a stolen
    ATM machine

Down main street   Or a body   flinging itself

From a train bridge   & the sparks   Lightswirl
    & the sparks

This is all about hunger, I said to the man next to me
    in the waiting room

Pointing at the bruises   Jesus Christ, he said,
    you should have seen it crawl

Back & beg   Even after we'd dropped cinder blocks
    on its face

& here you are   You are right fucking here

& the sparks   Here   & the sparks

Snow

i.

Ground hard as I-beams.
                    Blisters and whipping flags,

      but I can only remember how grandfather spat

      tobacco in Tupperware—sleet so cold I couldn't

      speak.

ii.

Today—a finger's calligraphy on car windows.

      Our ribs crack with longing.

      If I see you, I won't remember your name.

iii.

A poor taste on lips.   Tonight, a shattered cup.

                 The window breaks.

iv.

When the chest sweats, where is the light?   Cold, but
    face flushed like persimmons.

       Hold this. If it shakes, don't let go.

v.

I'm in love with sleeping bodies.
                I can't remember the melody.
                    I don't remember anything at all.

     Today, he brushed his teeth then leaped
     from the balcony.

     We couldn't hear over chiming glass, the snow
     falling straight down.

Who Finds You

I tar acres of wandering
The guarded woods hunting
Shudders of moonlight

My hands steadying
On barbed wire I open
My jacket to evening snow

The creases gleaming
My cheeks before
I shotgun myself in the face

And now I have fucked up
The voices are lightning
Jagged cracks in the frozen pond

And each holler beatboxes
Through the back-lit and feeble
Armed trees a reminder

That affliction is caress
Said over and over when
Your skin is lost to the cold

And in the moment before
The moment of noise everyone

Is eye to crotch in the delivery room
Of your panic they're rubbing IVs
Against their chests and picking
Their teeth with scalpels

While the sink overflows
With voice—will you follow
Into the dark but what is

That way the body suffers
Your eyes you are all wishless
And bewildered mouths of black

Berry fists pumping ribs they say
Come running with a star
Bright needle there is
Bound to be damage

*The gods are strange. They brew us fatal pleasures,
they use our virtues to betray us, they break our wings
across the wheel of loving.*

—EDWARD HIRSCH

Corpus

When I say *hello*, it means bite my heart.
Let the blackfly spin invisible & delirious

on vinyl. Let it save me from what I can't
know. Send posthumous letters in neon,

scribble love unreadable. My body is sweet
with blasphemy & punk teeth, memories

of slam-dancing underwater.
Tonight the absence of rain

is the mouth-open rush to noise:
a hurricane of wasps throat-clambering

for air. This half-earth where grind
sleeps dormant, a sickness without

temperature or cough. Hold my hand,
my nothing shouts. We'll stay up all night.

We'll orgy with shake and groove,
wet whisper—*clap, kiss, watch me go*.

Callnote

I stopped listening
as the blue jay hooked
its final turn.
I knew its business
was no longer air, only rage—
good just out of reach.
Jake, my nephew,
asked questions you hear
underwater. Questions answered
when a stranger ties your shoes.
We stared together. Everyone's
done this —gazed at an airplane
slicing sky & blossomed
with visions of balloons
bursting with gasoline. I held Jake
to the glass, bird in slow motion.
I squeezed his tiny hand
in time with *smack*.
Jake's bobbing head
drooled. The stain was a half-
finished Rothko. In the fading
light, the still bird was gray.
I wanted to take the window
out & frame it. I wanted
the delicate bones in my freezer.
I wanted to kiss Jake's soft head
& whisper—most days, this
is the sound of the world.

Fever

i.

Trample me   to the stage so I can hear   the butterfly
tongue the last   bee-swelled scream   Rats chewed

through   my night & now   I reverb with failure
        I am a bathroom stall sticky with a good

time's remains   During the coda
tell them it will be   painless   when   I'm gone

The crocuses are ablaze   Tell them   I can't be lonely
Tell them what   I buried   under the yew tree

ii.

if you need rock 'n' roll   stick a finger
in my chest   believe   the blackbirds
whistling   through my ribs
saw an ecstasy from my skull   savor

the slick-boned grit   split   me
open & a tanager   quivers to life
wing nailed to wing   it sings
the cripple   is the blind boy's

crayon-whipped   best   thump
its breast   & chuck me
in a dumpster   of needles
& rubber gloves   name this the big

bang   press a scalpel
through my cheek   & lick me
use your teeth   to scrape
the gravel   from my tongue

iii.

Skin searing blue-soft   I plunge
     in the hallway's spins   All strobe-lit

tits & teeth   I holler the bottle rocket
     I moan   There are secrets

carved into my pockmarked moon   Mouth my hurricane
     throat   I come Break me tender

I cry The glam-heart needs electric
     paint   I bleed   Stitch me shut at dawn

That First Day of Spring
Kind of Feeling

It's called the moonwalk. Front yard
glory. I eat frozen strawberries & watch

falling clouds, God's muscle-thick arms
whipping savage. All of us will hang for belief

in sunlight's rejuvenating power.
Today, I wear ditch cheeks, horse sparks

at my feet. Add wood chips to my pocket
lint & I have filthy thoughts. I itch melody.

Take away the frost, tremulous rhythm.
Sing breeze & I am an accordion

unbuttoning his jeans. Now is the season
to shave off my eyelids. Kiss me, ground,

I'll read you the dictionary backward.
A page a day for the rest of my life.

Look Close

Rain is holding its breath—water-damaging
The oatmealy clouds and you must want

To be the stranger of swollen doorways,
The specialist who cannot carve my insides

Enough. When you think midnight,
Do you taste hot honey and water

Or muffler-rust? When you hear thunder,
Remember the bowling balls herding

Around the buckled wood of your mother's home.
Bathroom light, womb-bright, the six-packs

Are slow tonight. There is a car smashing
Around my chest. Do you hear the breath

Of the waiting? It doesn't matter how
Many times we prick our tongues and touch.

Cocoon

No matter how well we live, there will be mornings
when 3,000 pounds of jet fuel spill from an airplane
racing across the sky. Every Tuesday a farmer falls
against a pitchfork in the barn. All of us will surprise
two bodies in a dark room, grinding each other soft,
or leave home in short sleeves on a day snowplows roar.
In one life or another, we've all been the pocket
of a murderer, restless with bullets, or a knotted sheet
tearing apart, unable to hold a lover's yearning weight.
Down the street, two boys are swinging behind the school.
In a week, one will be struck blind by the cry God makes
when someone lives. The same day, the other boy will write
the first sentence in his autobiography. It might be better
to be a caterpillar half-asleep on an elm branch, staring
marble-eyed at budding grass, but as soon as you think this,
the Saint of Ice Cubes pounds against your door.
Swaggering in his stillness, he looks you up and down,
pokes your chest. He makes you watch as, under the cashew
moon, he grins, rakes his cheek and yowls. Then, terrible
as the boy's soon-to-be-white eyes, he raises a fist
to the flickering streetlight and shakes wicked
the hummingbird he's squeezed into a bottle.

The Xylophone Is Blaze

Voltage or diabetic, my hands.
We crossed the river pirouetting

on buoys. Predictions of sunshine.
Come over now, my hands flutter.

Did you believe you were good
as the rust-dulled axe, the go-there-

be-happy? On a beach
of violin skins we turned into lightning,

or didn't, but smoked too fast,
attacking. Our chests tightened

with glee. Swaggering. Hip-tight
to the rough bark of perverted trees,

we shouted bloody, lips cowboy tall,
nick-winged & dusty.

I waited all day for you to tell me
that love is what I hate about myself.

Preface to Augury

In this place, beside a sigh of traffic,
Regretting nothing as it passes, there
Once was an endless trilling in a wood.
They say it, & saying it makes it so. —Larry Levis

I. Cardinal

I saw you kissing
the black pearls
in your reflection's eyes
& wanted to taste
the endless gift of a tire
filled with rainwater:
concentric circles
loosening themselves
from the throat-wrenching
grasp of the world.
Archimedic rhythm
that, when balanced,
turns you back
to red—a heart
bursting in flutter
above a chain-link fence.
Turned inside
out & pulsing
sugary—thick smoke
in summer air.

II. Oriole

After the storm,
the horsehair nest
you weaved lay frayed
on the bottom step
like a nail-filled sock.
For weeks, I crunched
the retort of fallen branches,
gathered newspapers
from towns hours away.
By the time I restaked
the vine's bamboo poles,
the comb you'd stolen
from the bathroom window
was tucked in the tree's V—
mother's gray hairs
unfurled into the air
like a night photo
of fireworks.
Two days later
the comb shined new.
You disappeared into
the lassoed tornado,
hiding your plumage
in a privacy where anything
could happen: promises
of wheat fields smoking
like pyres, tomato plants

pecked in the fibrous dark.
What do you name in your
never-ending shade?
Which sacrifice is true loss?
Veiled, a song rattling
the knob-shouldered sumac.
Fork-lightning, fire; raw-throated
through the orchard's cobalt day.

III. Magpie

Do you save
the best for last
like I do? Eyes
taken first, rib cage
scoured white.
The squirrel's belly
must be tender
for you to pick
cruelly all day
with your dagger face.
Reminder of night's
warm sidewalks,
you are a shadow
in pawnshop alleys.
Watching
from the stop sign,
morning legs
exclamation marks
against the rising sun.
You predict scars,
count soft parts
like a gambler
already spending
his winnings.
Surer than hell
he'll taste the queen's
sweaty kiss
after his double down.

Sophisticated

Spin with me, flamenco-style.

Here—a boutonniere weaved from tender split nails.

I am a three-winged angel, graceful with my fingertips.

My sound, the small particles of prophecy.

Do you believe and stay attached
to your small desires, old fruits,
or do you want to lie down?

It could be foam-white,
the *I cannot remember* room
or your eyes are white as the clown
fish's belly. Here is the highway

to the lumpy bed, moldy
with floodwater, headboards
carved from church organs.

It is not necessary to sleep.

The shortcut is closed, laced steely with daytime.

I am here to help. Flares, a white flag.

Siphon gas from my lungs, spread my jelly and sing.

I am one fraction away.

One one-hundredth from what will make all the difference.

Below the Nearer Sky

The goldfish sprints, fantail
spread like fingers on fire.

It fast-forwards for days—
figure-eights a whirling fury

that spills. Spinning drunkenly,
everything is forgotten. It burns,

a lightning-struck barn.
Its silken flesh unfurls, ribs

shine like a whittled moon.
But skin knotted into ruin

can't stop it: the staccato jazz
your fingernail flicks doesn't help.

It will never quit, you think,
until the summer morning

it's found belly-up in dirty water,
still as a town ravaged by storm.

The fishbowl shimmers dark and golden
as if, in your absence, the heavens

crawled in—packed star chunks
cellophane tight; waiting for you

to shake off your impossible dreams
and bow to that half-whole reflection.

Happy Fun Sex Movie

Night light rubbing & riffraff.
Singing waxed violence, sky sharp
as razors & fortuitous.

Nibble my nape. My snappiness.
I've been blue-foxed, led shackled
to solitary confinement in a field

planted with mimes. With darts.
They tickle my larynx.
Sickly with cracked lobes.

Is it selfish to want
the salted & tart?
Head table at the hello

party? Dip. Dab. Drip.
Cracked open, shell
a tumored morning. Gongs.

Leave the checkered neck.
Leave my selfishness.
Let the chokecherry paint,

let it sputter everyone righteous.
Babies sprout from the chili vine.
We are so beautiful in this eeldom.

Tumult

The kill, the tongue in my throat.

—Mary Wang

After these days dense
with whoops & catcalls,

blizzards of oystered glass
& whippoorwills barking out

oddness, I walk in my sleep.
A murder of intimacies worrying

my throat tarnished. Shackled
to slamming doors, I've given myself

wholly to the city's ragtag
roughness. Dreams of exaltation

line power lines like shooting
decoys. Swabbed for electrocution.

They alternate intrusion.
They alternate blessings.

And each morning, the terrible
biography writes across the sky.

ACKNOWLEDGMENTS

Thank you thank you thank you to everyone at Macalester College and the creative writing program at the University of Minnesota—flowers and Band-Aids to all of my students, colleagues, and peers. Wang Ping, Diane Glancy, Ray Gonzalez, Rick Barot, David Hernandez, Lisa Glatt, Adam Clay, Casey Golden, Suzanne Rivecca, Matt Henriksen, Mark Conway, and Nick Flynn, thank you for the guidance, doom, and help.

I am also grateful to the National Endowment for the Arts, the Minnesota State Arts Board, SASE/Jerome, Iowa Falls, and Dr. Roberto Heros, for supporting this life.

Forever: I am indebted to the beautiful people at Tin House. Thank you for believing in me, Brenda. Thank you for putting up with me, Meg.

Finally, I owe everything and more to my families (Lemon, McLoone, Dorlac, Garlock, Balizet, and Ariane & Catface) and friends. I love you all.